SAVORING GOD'S LOVE

25 DEVOTIONS for WOMEN

Jane Wilke

How sweet are your words to my taste.

Psalm 119:103 NLT

www.CTAinc.com

Savoring God's Love
by Jane Wilke

Copyright © 2006 by CTA, Inc.
1625 Larkin Williams Rd.
Fenton, MO 63026-1205

Unless otherwise indicated, Scripture quotations are from the HOLY BIBLE, NEW INTERNATIONAL VERSION®. Copyright © 1973, 1978, 1984 International Bible Society. Used by permission of Zondervan. All rights reserved.

Scripture quotations so indicated are from THE MESSAGE. Copyright © by Eugene H. Peterson 1993, 1994, 1995, 1996, 2000, 2001, 2002. Used by permission of NavPress Publishing Group.

Scripture quotations marked NLT are taken from the Holy Bible, New Living Translation, copyright © 1996. Used by permission of Tyndale House Publishers, Inc., Wheaton, Illinois 60189. All rights reserved.

The herbs on the cover are chives, basil, and hyssop.

ISBN 1-933234-09-1

PRINTED IN THAILAND

E ach devotion throughout this booklet will help you savor one particularly powerful description of our Savior's love as you examine in depth the words of Romans 5:1–5, 8. Here they are in their entirety. May you find them sweet—sweeter than honey! And may God the Holy Spirit use these words to strengthen your heart in love for your Savior!

Therefore, since we have been justified through faith, we have peace with God through our Lord Jesus Christ, through whom we have gained access by faith into this grace in which we now stand. And we rejoice in the hope of the glory of God. Not only so, but we also rejoice in our sufferings, because we know that suffering produces perseverance; perseverance, character; and character, hope. And hope does not disappoint us, because God has poured out his love into our hearts by the Holy Spirit, whom he has given us. . . . But God demonstrates his own love for us in this: While we were still sinners, Christ died for us.

Romans 5:1–8

Day 1

Your words are so choice, so tasty.

Psalm 119:103 THE MESSAGE

I have a friend who has an herb garden—her front yard, back yard, and windowsills are all adorned with savory herbs. Like an artist preparing a masterpiece, she knows how each one can add just the right touch to flavor various recipes she prepares. And this flavoring, of course, makes it possible for her guests to savor those foods!

I've always admired the spice connoisseur, the cook who can make an ordinary dish explode with hidden flavors. When something tastes *extra*-ordinary, it invites more than mere tasting, it invites savoring. Small bites, slow bites, lolling-over-the-taste-buds kind of lingering. We savor so that the pleasure associated with the taste will last—and last.

That's what each reading in this devotional booklet is designed to help you do—to go beyond mere tasting. In order to truly savor a fantastic dessert, for example, you would take your time in the eating, breaking off small bites and enjoying them one at a time. That's what we will be doing here, too—taking a reading from Scripture and breaking it into smaller phrases for our deliberation and delight. In doing so, you can savor each word. You can make sure you don't miss the delightful sweetness of your Savior's love, his love for you in this particular place and time in your life.

When a person thinks about eating merely in terms of survival, that person will rarely savor the flavor of food. What pleasure that person misses! Similarly, if you look at your devotional reading as a mere routine, you will miss much of the pleasure in being with your Lord and basking in his love. Pause instead. Take time to savor God's Word. Let the Holy Spirit use it to shape you into the person he longs for you to become. Let God take what you know in your head and move it to a place in your heart where it can begin to flavor your life with meaning. Then you will truly savor the Savior's love for you!

TO SAVOR

Meditate on the verse below as you pray about its meaning right now. Let the sweetness of your Lord's undeserved favor in the cross of his Son encourage and strengthen you.

> *Let the word of Christ dwell in you richly. . . . And whatever you do, whether in word or deed, do it all in the name of the Lord Jesus, giving thanks to God the Father through him.*
>
> Colossians 3:16–17

TO FLAVOR

We describe some spices as tangy, some as hot, some as cool, some as bitter. Not many fall into the "sweet" category. Perhaps that's why Scripture often compares God's Word to honey. Wild honey, plentiful in the Holy Land ("a land flowing with milk and honey"), was commonly used to flavor fried cakes and as a treat to spread on barley bread.

—Chives

Day 2

Since we have been justified . . .

Romans 5:1

E xfoliation. Years ago, I didn't even know that word existed. Now I've added it to my vocabulary. Since reaching the age at which I must work to de-age my skin, I find myself aware that skin cells regenerate themselves and that I can help the process along by sloughing away the top layer of dead skin cells. Sounds appetizing, doesn't it?

I recently came across a sea scrub that most certainly does the trick. It's hard to believe I'm admitting to this, but it feels great! If only I could do that with the dead, rough places in my emotional and spiritual life—those areas that need clearing away—the hurts, the scars, the fears, the tears.

Sadly, nothing I can do will accomplish this—no exfoliating sea scrub will make that kind of damage disappear. Why? Because each results from sin, my own sin and the sins by which others have hurt me. Sin always separates, always ruins relationships. Humanity's right relationship with God was broken with the first sin in the Garden of Eden. And nothing any of us can do on our own will ever restore the rightness of that relationship.

Yet today's text from Romans 5 tells us that we have been "justified." A strange word, isn't it? A few years ago, I heard a simple, yet profound, explanation of what it means. When Christ died on the cross, it was "just [as] if I'd" died on the cross. In other words, Christ died as my substitute. Because Christ took your place and mine upon the cross, God declares us just, or righteous, and forgiven. The relationship is restored. And the old becomes new!

TO SAVOR

Meditate on the verse below as you pray about the joy and freedom this truth creates in your heart!

You forgave the guilt of my sin.

Psalm 32:5

TO FLAVOR

Basil has an enchanting fragrance with hints of mint, licorice, and clove. It brings excitement to a number of dishes. At its peak in summer, it goes especially well with summer vegetables and tomatoes.

~Chives

Day 3

We have peace.

Romans 5:1

O ne day while traveling in Alaska, I walked into a small antique shop where a unique table caught my eye. I left it there in the shop; I was miles away from home and the practical side of me won out—to ship it seemed, well, impractical.

At first I found myself puzzled by its appeal. Then, finally, I figured it out. The table's mosaic top was made of broken pieces of glass. The artisan who made it had captured many broken pieces and fitted them together to form a beautiful design.

Then I realized the tabletop pictured my own life. Much has been wrong. Much has gone wrong. Much has shattered my peace and broken my life into pieces. Those pieces of broken hope could have lain forever splintered, forever wounding my heart. But because of Jesus, they have not. The Master Artisan has fashioned each sliver, piece-by-piece, forming a beautiful mosaic, a lovely design first conceived in the heart of God himself!

How do you describe peace? Peace isn't the absence of trouble, for trouble will always be part of the brokenness sin brings into our lives here on earth. Rather, true peace lives and grows from deep within hearts that cling to Christ as Savior. Only when the peace of Christ thrives deep within does it begin to show on the outside as we interact with others in our day-to-day lives. As the Holy Spirit creates and nourishes a faith relationship with God in our hearts, true peace blooms as a by-product. We find that peace only in Christ who says, "Peace I leave with you; my peace I give you" (John 14:27).

> *No God, no peace.*
> *Know God, know peace.*

Author unknown

TO SAVOR

Let these words strengthen your sense of peace, no matter what your outward circumstances today.

> *Now may the Lord of peace himself give you peace at all times and in every way.*

2 Thessalonians 3:16

TO FLAVOR

Bay leaves impart a great flavor but are not generally eaten by themselves. They dispense their flavor throughout long simmering, so they are best used in stocks, stews, and sauces.

~Chives

Day 4

Peace with God . . .

Romans 5:1

Have you ever tried to repair a broken relationship, to erase the bitterness between yourself and someone else, only to have your words and the effort seem superficial—even to you? Most likely, you were only giving the reconciliation "lip service," doing and saying what you knew you should, but continuing to harbor resentment in your heart. Without forgiveness, it is impossible to restore that which is broken in a relationship.

The same is true of our relationship with God our Father. Sin broke it apart and without forgiveness, we could never be right with God. Without forgiveness, we could never truly be at peace with God. But thanks be to God that the gift of forgiveness is ours through Christ. Not only can we find peace *in* him, but we can also find peace *with* him.

Though we had offended a holy God, Jesus Christ opened the path of reconciliation. Far, far beyond mere lip service, he paid for our sins with his own blood. We can approach God with our fears and tears; we can now lay down the burdens of our hearts and souls, fully assured that he will carry them for us and grant us *his* peace.

Nor all my prayers nor sighs or tears
Can ease my awful load.

> *Thy work alone, O Christ,*
> *Can ease this weight of sin;*
> *Thy blood alone, O Lamb of God,*
> *Can give me peace within.*

Horatius Bonar

TO SAVOR

Rest in Jesus' gifts of forgiveness and love as you savor today's verse, praying over it and thinking deeply about it.

> *Come to me, all you who are weary and burdened, and I will give you rest.*

Matthew 11:28

TO FLAVOR

Chives are edible on their own and offer a mild onion flavor. They hold their flavor best when cooked very little or not at all. Be sure to use only fresh chives; drying takes away all flavor.

~Chives

Day 5

Through our Lord Jesus Christ. . .

Romans 5:1

What is it about friendships between women—the bond that holds women together, even as years pass by? UCLA conducted a landmark research study that produced surprising results on this very topic. It tied a hormone called oxytocin to this phenomenon, stating that when this hormone is released in women as part of the stress response, it influences us to turn to tending and befriending. Therefore, the study concludes, friendships with other women can calm stress, keep us healthy, and perhaps even add years to our lives.

Friendship most certainly is a source of strength and nurture, especially when we find a friend in whom we can truly confide— one who listens, who nudges when necessary, who forgives. Yet friendships can be stretched and even broken, filled with bitter disappointment and unmet expectations. After all, no friend could ever be perfect in our imperfect world. Right? Wrong!

We have one perfect friend, a friend who listens, nudges, and forgives—each time—always, and forever. That friend is our Lord and Savior, Jesus Christ. In John 15:12–17, Jesus calls his disciples his friends . . . and he does the same for you and me.

Like the disciples, we know we do not deserve such love, such friendship, for we will always fall short of his expectations. We will always let him down. But our Savior's love and forgiveness are unconditional. He is there for us and will continue to be there for us through eternity. How's that for an antidote to stress?

— TO SAVOR —

Let joy flood your heart as you remember Jesus, your truest friend today, meditating on his words:

> *[Jesus said,] You are my friends if you do what I command. . . . This is my command: Love each other.*
>
> John 15:14, 17

— TO FLAVOR —

Dill might look feathery light, but its flavor packs a punch. Toss some in at the end of cooking and you'll be delighted by how it perks up your dishes—especially vegetable dishes.

—*Chives*

The Most Essential Ingredient

TO FLAVOR

If we're truly honest, most of us will have to admit that we use herbs and spices without a completely clear idea of what effects they'll have on food. Some herbs can be used together; others are best used alone. We can toss some by the handful into the pot; for others, just a pinch will do.

To use herbs and spices expertly, to create foods worth savoring, means we need to get to know them—to experiment, to experience some failures, and to celebrate some successes.

Isn't that the same in our spiritual lives? Sometimes we add a pinch of prayer to our day and mix it with a large dose of studying his Word. Sometimes, it's the other way around. At other times, it's a little of both.

But how can we truly learn to savor the Savior's love unless we learn to know him more intimately?

TO SAVOR

Think for a bit about the relationship you've had with Christ up to this point in your life. Use the space provided to write a letter to your Savior; express your feelings about how you've come to know him and your thoughts and feelings about getting to know him more intimately.

_____

_____

_____

_____

_____

_____

_____

_____

_____

_____

_____

_____

_____

FOR THE SAVIOR

Lord, draw me ever closer to you. Awaken my senses and touch my heart. Stir up in me a hunger and thirst for your Word. In your name I pray, Lord Jesus. Amen.

Day 6

Through whom we have gained access by faith . . .

Romans 5:2

How many passwords do you have to remember? It used to be that passwords belonged exclusively to the realm of secret clubs in childhood, passwords like "No Boys Allowed!" But now, we use them every day. We need them to open most computer software programs. Then we need them to access our Internet browser, and we need them again when we want to enter into that favorite Web site for browsing or buying who knows what. Even if we're not computer literate, we use PIN numbers with our debit card at the grocery store or when we place an order with our favorite mail-order company.

Passwords give us access; without them we would be locked out. Thus the importance of remembering our passwords. I don't know about you, but at just the wrong moment, I tend to forget which password I need. My feelings in those moments fall somewhere between panic and annoyance.

None of this applies as we think about access to our Father in heaven. He will never lock us out, and we never have to remember a password. Our access to heaven's throne room does not depend upon anything we do. We enjoy free and limitless access because of what our Savior, Jesus, has done for us. He has wiped clean the slate of our sin. He has opened the way to the Father. By faith in what Jesus did on a hill called Calvary, we access the listening ear of the God who created the universe!

The reformer Martin Luther once said, "Faith is permitting ourselves to be seized by the things we do not see." We may not see or feel it, but God is holding his hand out to us. Grab hold in faith, and you will not be disappointed.

TO SAVOR

What does Romans 5:2 mean for you as an individual? for your family? neighborhood? church? Ponder it today as you also savor these words:

[Jesus said,] "I am the way and the truth and the life."

John 14:6

TO FLAVOR

Marjoram has a flavor similar to thyme, and so it can be used to replace thyme if necessary. If you use it fresh, add it toward the end of your cooking time. Otherwise, it will lose some of its flavor. If you are using dried marjoram, add it to your ingredients early in the cooking process to release the maximum flavor.

~Marigold

Day 7

Into this grace . . .

Romans 5:2

T he story is told of an English fisherman who, after a long, hard day, entered an inn and ordered a pot of tea. In a moment of bravado (bragging about his huge catch of fish), he dramatically swept his arm to one side and proceeded to knock the teapot off the table. As he did so, he also splashed a dark stain across the wallpaper.

Horrified and dismayed, the fisherman apologized profusely and tried to wipe off the tea, but he only made the stain worse. Right then, a stranger quietly rose from the table next to the fisherman and produced a coal pencil. He used it to sketch around the stain. In but a few moments, he created a magnificent stallion that looked as though it belonged at that very spot on the wall. Patrons at the inn soon recognized the artist as Sir Edmond Lancier, England's foremost painter of wildlife.

What Lancier did with the fisherman's unsightly stain, God does for each of us every day of our lives. By the ugly things we have said and done, we have earned only punishment. But because our Savior sacrificed himself on our behalf, we are made new. God himself is creating a masterpiece out of our ruined lives. We do not deserve this great gift; therefore, Scripture calls the gift "grace."

Savor the words from the much-loved song below. Then talk with Jesus about the wonderful words of Romans 3:24 as you savor your Lord's love for you!

> *Turn your eyes upon Jesus,*
> *Look full in his wonderful face,*
> *And the things of the earth will grow strangely dim,*
> *In the light of his glory and grace.*

Helen H. Lemmel

TO SAVOR

[We] are justified freely by his grace through the redemption that came by Christ Jesus.

Romans 3:24

TO FLAVOR

Mint grows in over 60 varieties, but the one most often used as an herb is spearmint. Peppermint, on the other hand, is most often used to flavor candies and desserts. Good cooks use mint with a variety of meats, sauces, vegetables, and fruits.

~Marigold

Day 8

In which we now stand . . .

Romans 5:2

One day my husband and I headed into the theater to see a movie. It would start in a few minutes, and so I quickly strode around the corner—and ran headlong into another woman. Already a bit unsteady on her feet, she was walking with a cane. I instantly reached for her hands while at the same time stepping back with one foot, and in this way steadying myself. While others waited to catch her from behind, I'm thankful I can say I was able to pull her upright. But without the secure footing I established, we both might have sprawled onto the floor!

How strong is your stance—spiritually speaking? Much like the roots of stately trees that have weathered years of storms, we can stand firm in the promises of God. And in those promises, we find an anchor that transforms our lives. By faith in our Savior who lived, died, and rose again for us, our lives set roots down deep in the unchanging love of God. We enjoy free and full forgiveness of all our sins through faith in Jesus Christ, our Savior.

God has sealed that promise in his grace. In his hymn "Jesus, Lover of My Soul," Charles Wesley wrote this beautiful line: "Reach me out Thy gracious hand, while I of Thy strength receive." Christ Jesus has already reached out to you, he is holding you, and he will keep you standing firm!

TO SAVOR

Ponder the power and comfort in this promise of God, a promise he makes afresh—to you—today!

> *You will keep in perfect peace him whose mind is steadfast, because he trusts in you.*
>
> *Isaiah 26:3*

TO FLAVOR

Oregano boasts a strong, pungent flavor. It dries well and the longer it dries, the more its flavor improves. Use it especially to flavor any dish that features tomatoes and cheese (e.g., pizza, spaghetti sauce, chili).

~Marigold

Day 9

And we rejoice.

My dad lay dying. Just as cancer had ushered my mom into heaven, so now it was doing the same for Dad. I lived 500 miles away, and so every few weeks I came home to spend time beside him. One morning he asked me to read to him from the Bible. So I did what perhaps you yourself have sometimes done; I opened to read a chapter from whatever page happened to fall open in my dad's well-worn Bible.

As I began to read Psalm 118, I marveled at how the words took on new meaning! "I will not die but live" (verse 17). "Open for me the gates of righteousness; I will enter and give thanks to the LORD" (verse 19). And then came the verse that really spoke to my heart: "This is the day the LORD has made; let us rejoice and be glad in it" (verse 24).

Rejoicing . . . even amidst suffering. That's what Dad was modeling for me—a joy that went deeper than the hoopla we so often associate with happiness. Dad was rejoicing in a lifetime of blessings his heavenly Father had poured out upon him. He could rejoice in complete confidence, total assurance. His Savior stood beside him, ready to welcome him home.

The psalmist rejoiced over deliverance made possible by Christ's victory over sin and death. So did my dad. And so can you. The trials that could bring you down today are but temporary. Christ's victory on Calvary and in his open tomb is your victory . . . and that victory is eternal!

TO SAVOR

When do you find it most difficult to rejoice in Jesus? Ponder that today as you reflect on these words of the apostle Paul:

> *Be joyful always; pray continually; give thanks in all circumstances, for this is God's will for you in Christ Jesus.*
>
> 1 Thessalonians 5:16–18

TO FLAVOR

Parsley goes well with most everything, though it is often relegated to the edge of the plate, simply to add a colorful garnish. Use it as soon as possible after picking it and be sure to rinse it completely. When chewed, parsley stems will freshen breath.

~Marigold

Day 10

In the hope . . .

Romans 5:2

The sky never falls, no matter how hard it rains.
God's love never fails, regardless of your pains.

Author unknown

Remember the story of Chicken Little? Let me refresh your memory. One day as she was walking in the woods, an acorn fell on her head. Leaping to a conclusion, she ran to tell all her friends, "The sky is falling; the sky is falling! We must tell the king!"

In her dismay, she convinced Henny Penny, Cocky Locky, and Goosey Loosey to join her. The wiser Foxy Woxy took advantage of the four friends' fear, luring them into the woods under the pretense of pointing out a shortcut. But the king sent his dogs to the rescue, and from that day on, Chicken Little carried around an umbrella (a present from the king) to protect her from errant acorns.

How many times have I acted like Chicken Little, assuming my world was falling apart around me? How many times have I convinced family and friends of the same? And how many times has Satan taken advantage of my fear, deceiving me into thinking I could take a shortcut to safety? In my own case, I'm afraid, it's been too many times to count. How about you?

PAGE 24
SAVORING GOD'S LOVE

Still, time after time, Christ my King comes to the rescue. Living a holy life and dying an agonizing death in my place, Jesus has accomplished my ultimate rescue, saving me from an eternity of separation from God. But his love doesn't stop there. He knows me in my weakness as I live here in this life. He knows my tendency to see only as far as my fears, and so he offers me an umbrella of hope—hope secure and certain, hope that knows God's love in Christ, hope forever strong enough to protect and comfort me in any and every situation.

TO SAVOR

Is today a rainy day for you? Let the Holy Spirit work hope in your heart through the truth of this verse:

God is our refuge and strength, an ever-present help in trouble.

Psalm 46:1

TO FLAVOR

Rosemary carries a very strong flavor and scent. Add dried rosemary leaves early in the cooking process to give them time to soften. Use rosemary with lamb, pork, and chicken. Try it also in tomato soups and sauces.

—*Marigold*

Which Is Which?

TO FLAVOR

So what's the difference between an herb and a spice? Herbalists tend to use both as health enhancers or remedies for health problems, lumping herbs and spices into one category—whether plants, plant extracts, or plant preparations. For herbalists, bulbs, spices, leaves, and even bark fall in the same category. But for cooking, there *is* a difference.

Both herbs and spices come from plants, sometimes even from the same plant. Herbs used in cooking are typically taken from the leaves of the plant (e.g., basil, cilantro, tarragon). But spices come from just about any part of the plant *except* the leaves. For example, seeds (e.g., fennel), seed pods (e.g., cardamom), flowers (e.g., saffron), berries (e.g., juniper), buds (e.g., cloves), and even bark (e.g., cinnamon).

To many people in our world today, God can be many things: a spiritual center, a force living within, a general sense of well-being, and many other things. But don't be confused—the only true God is the God who sent his own Son to be our Savior, Jesus. Only the one, true, triune God loves us with a love that forgives all sin, heals all hurts, and lasts into all eternity. There *is* a difference.

TO SAVOR

Imagine you just met someone who asked, "Who is Jesus?" What would you say?

_____

_____

_____

_____

_____

_____

_____

_____

_____

_____

_____

_____

FOR THE SAVIOR

Lord, fill me with the sense of joy and peace that only you can provide. Help me to stand firm in my faith in you—my one, true, faithful God. May I always look to you as the source of my strength from day to day. In the name of Jesus, my Savior. Amen.

Day 11

Of the glory of God . . .

Romans 5:2

I f I could choose to meet in person anyone in the world, present or past, I think I'd choose Corrie ten Boom. Her story of faith and forgiveness in the face of the Nazi holocaust truly inspires me. After seeing her father and sister die, and after having herself survived the horrors of the Ravensbruck concentration camp, Corrie went on to touch the entire world with her story.

Yet it wasn't *her* story; it was *his*-story. History recounts what happened to Corrie, to be sure. But the story she went on to tell was that of the faithfulness of God's love, faithfulness that gave her hope in a seemingly hopeless situation. Some of her "lost writings" have been compiled into a book titled *Reflections of God's Glory*. In these writings, she shares the truth that God has placed us here to be mirrors of his glory. Her words reflect those of 2 Corinthians 3:18.

> *And we, who with unveiled faces all reflect the Lord's glory,*
> *are being transformed into his likeness with ever-increasing glory,*
> *which comes from the Lord, who is the Spirit.*

Corrie comments, "You may feel that your character, your circumstances, your experience are anything but a growing process of being transformed into the likeness of Jesus, continually becoming more and more of a mirror of the glory of the Lord . . . [but] the power which enables him to bring everything under his control is strong enough for him to take you and me . . . by the hand."

Can you relate? His-story . . . His glory!

— TO SAVOR —

As you reflect on how you will mirror the glory of God today, let this verse guide your thoughts and actions:

So whether you eat or drink or whatever you do, do it all for the glory of God.

1 Corinthians 10:31

— TO FLAVOR —

Sage is best known for its use in holiday stuffing, but its strong, musty flavor can enhance meat and poultry any time of year. It goes well in many soups and tomato sauces. If you use dry sage, take care to add it sparingly.

—Lungwort

Day 12

But we also rejoice . . .

Romans 5:3

At one time or another, perhaps you have participated in some sort of brainstorming session. In order to get the creative ideas flowing, no doubt your group's leader set some ground rules, welcoming all ideas, urging that no one object to anyone else's ideas, and advocating for a "yes, and" (rather than a "no, but") approach. A "yes, and" attitude opens possibilities.

That's why, as I read today's verse, I find myself wanting to replace *but* with *yes, and.* I want the words to read, "Yes, and we also rejoice. . ." Yet even as I make that replacement, I feel the "but" coming, the objections rising in my heart as I get ready to turn a corner in my thoughts.

So what corner will we turn here? Earlier in this passage, we found ourselves rejoicing "in the hope of the glory of God" (Romans 5:2). So then, what will come next? The good . . . the bad . . . the ugly? Perhaps any of these or all of these! Or perhaps the secret lies in how we look at the circumstances of our lives. Do we see in those circumstances a random collection of knots and haphazard threads? Or do we turn the tapestry over to reveal the masterpiece of our Lord's design?

The apostle writes, "No eye has seen, no ear has heard, no mind has conceived what God has prepared for those who love him" (1 Corinthians 2:9). In other words, God wants to do more in our lives than we could ever imagine. Think of it! He even sent his own Son to die for us! Because that's true, we can hang on for the "yes, and" circumstances that lie just around the next corner!

— TO SAVOR —

When we lose sight of what God has prepared for us, we also lose our joy. Consider that—and pray about it—as you consider today's verse to ponder:

We have come to share in Christ if we hold firmly till the end the confidence we had at first.

Hebrews 3:14

— TO FLAVOR —

Thyme combines well with many other herbs and spices. Expert cooks use it both fresh and dried. It's hard to name a dish that thyme will not enhance. Try it with rice, grains, dried beans, meats, and poultry.

~Lungwort

Day 13

. . . in our sufferings . . .

Romans 5:3

D o you remember the old rag rugs of years gone by? What a great reminder of a spiritual, scriptural truth: In Christ, God gathers the ragged pieces of our lives, the pieces we ourselves might very well want to discard. He weaves them into a work of dignity and purpose—a work that reflects his glory. Psalm 34:18 tells us that "the LORD is close to the brokenhearted and saves those who are crushed in spirit."

What is crushing your spirit these days? What is it that is causing you to ask, Why me? Why now? Why this? Only one person can fully answer all your whys, but the inspired words of the apostle Paul offer some great insight. Paraphrased, 2 Corinthians 1:3–7 says:

What a wonderful God we have—He is the Father of our Lord Jesus Christ, the source of mercy, the one who comforts and strengthens us in every hardship and trial. Why? So that when others are troubled, needing encouragement, we can pass on to them this same help and comfort God has given to us.

Our Savior, who experienced the most devastating suffering possible on our behalf—total separation from the Father—stands beside us now and forever to comfort us in all our distresses. Knowing his presence, we also can trust his promise to use even the most troubling of circumstances to accomplish his purposes in our lives. We may feel tattered and torn by life, but our Savior can use even the rags of our experiences to weave a tapestry of praise!

TO SAVOR

Pray each individual word or phrase from Romans 8:28 as you ask the Holy Spirit to strengthen your confidence in his love and faithfulness.

> *We know that in all things God works for the good of those who love him, who have been called according to his purpose.*
>
> Romans 8:28

TO FLAVOR

Allspice includes a mixture of a variety of spices—cloves, cinnamon, nutmeg, and even black pepper! The spice is usually ground like pepper. Good cooks use it as a perfect all-purpose spice for baking.

~Lungwort

Day 14

Suffering produces perseverance . . .

Romans 5:3

My husband and I received a silver tea set as a wedding present. Not one to use it very often, I find myself having to remove the tarnish and polish the silver whenever such an occasion arises. Each time, I am amazed at how the silver begins to reflect my image as I polish.

No doubt you have heard or read about articles or devotions in which the author compares the work God does in times of trouble with the process of refining silver. The Scripture itself often makes this same comparison. In Psalm 66, for instance, the psalmist recalls God's merciful deliverances and reflects on the Lord's praiseworthiness in these words: "For you, O God, tested us; you refined us like silver" (verse 10).

Not long ago, I learned that silversmiths must hold a piece of silver in the midst of a fire, right where the flames are hottest, in order to burn away completely all the impurities. Yet a master silversmith must keep an eye on the silver the entire time, for left in the flames too long, it would be destroyed. How does the silversmith know when to remove his masterpiece from the heat? When it reflects his image!

Is God holding you, his masterpiece, in the fire of trouble right now? The great hymn "How Firm a Foundation" puts this analogy into perspective, reminding us of God's faithfulness to us throughout the process.

When through fiery trials your pathway shall lie,
My grace, all-sufficient, will be your supply.
The flame shall not hurt you;
I only design your dross to consume and your gold to refine.

John Rippon

TO SAVOR

When do you have the hardest time believing your Lord has only your good in mind—no matter how severe your pain or how deep your loss? Keep his refining purposes in mind as you ponder this promise:

"I know the plans I have for you," declares the LORD, "plans to prosper you and not to harm you, plans to give you hope and a future."

Jeremiah 29:11

TO FLAVOR

Cardamom commonly comes as a dry powder or a small pod. Its larger pods are very strong. In its powdered form, cardamom tastes great in sweet breads, muffins, and buttery cookies. It's also a wonderful complement to most fruits.

—Lungwort

Day 15

. . . perseverance, character . . .

Romans 5:4

I'm sure you've seen them—those posters with the incredible pictures and the inspirational phrases intended to motivate and offer insight. Here are two of my favorites: "Attitude is a little thing that makes a BIG difference" and "Character is who you are when only God is watching."

It's not exactly a newsflash. We live in a world wracked with sin. That fact leads to another: life comes with trouble and pain. When faced with a new problem, most of us try to find a way out, but sometimes that's not possible. Sometimes the trials we face grow out of the choices of others: a child's rebellion, a spouse's betrayal, the unexpected devastation of losing a job. You may not be able to change your circumstances, but you can control the ways you respond to those circumstances.

Many things that happen in life are not fair; living in triumph amidst difficulty requires that we focus our strength and energy on releasing ourselves to God and letting him protect, comfort, and counsel us through the struggle. When we do that, anger, bitterness, sadness, and self-pity will not set down their roots in our hearts.

We see Christ himself in the Garden of Gethsemane asking the Father to take the cup of suffering and death from him. But Jesus could not avoid what lay ahead. As he trusted the Father's wisdom and released himself to the Father's care, God turned the tables on the powers and principalities that sought to destroy his Son. Now, through faith in Jesus as our Savior, Jesus' victory belongs to us!

We pray that this trust, worked in us by our Lord, will shine forth in our character.

TO SAVOR

Each verse this week has encouraged us to cling in confidence to a trustworthy God, the one who loves us and has saved us through the suffering of his Son. Consider this truth one last time this week as you meditate on these words:

> *Trust in the LORD with all your heart and lean not on your own understanding; in all your ways acknowledge him, and he will make your paths straight.*

Proverbs 3:5–6

TO FLAVOR

Celery seeds come in handy when you want a taste of celery but can't use this vegetable itself (e.g., in biscuits, muffins, crackers). You can use celery seed to complement the taste of eggs, fish, and many soups.

—Lungwort

When Stronger Is Better

TO FLAVOR

If you are like me, you may have always assumed that fresh herbs taste better than dried. We've been conditioned to think that fresher is better, but that's not always so—at least not with herbs. Often, dried herbs are just as good, and sometimes they're even better!

For example, some herbs can be chewy when fresh—certainly unpleasant if you happen to get an entire mouthful. Also, adding fresh herbs too early in the cooking process can rob them of their flavor and color. Dried herbs are, in most cases, stronger and tougher—so much so that you have to be careful to not use too much. A teaspoon of some dried herbs can create flavor as strong as an entire tablespoon of that same herb when used fresh!

So in terms of herbs, an herb that's gone through the drying process can flavor better and last longer. Isn't the same true for us? Aren't we stronger for all the life experiences God has, in grace, seen us through?

TO SAVOR

Think back to a time when your Lord Jesus has used a challenge or hardship to make you stronger. What did you learn about his love during this time? What did the Holy Spirit teach you about you? about himself?

_____

_____

_____

_____

_____

_____

_____

_____

_____

_____

_____

_____

_____

FOR THE SAVIOR

Lord, mold me and shape me. Help me learn to look to you for guidance and to trust your leading. Teach me to be thankful in all circumstances. Then use me to share the comfort of your love with others in their times of trouble. In the name of Jesus, my Savior. Amen.

Day 16

. . . and character, hope.

Romans 5:4

E arly in my career, I taught preschoolers. During those years, Groundhog Day gave my students and me many fun opportunities to play with our own shadows. The children found it hard to grasp the concept at first. I found it delightful to watch as individual children tried to outsmart their shadow. After awhile, each child would figure out that whenever the sun was in front them, their shadow would be behind them.

Helen Keller once said, "Keep your face to the sunshine, and you cannot see the shadows." Disappointment. Anxiety. Self-doubt. Worry. Anger. Guilt. We encounter shadows like these day by day as we live here on earth. Do shadows like these ever plague you? Do you ever try to outsmart them?

Most of us would like to chase away life's shadows and find a way to prevent their return. But much like children whistling into the darkness as they walk past a cemetery, we find our fears and anxieties returning again and again. As long as we live in this present creation, marred as it is by sin, we will find our own sin and the sins of those around us troublesome.

Thank God for our Savior, Jesus Christ, who faced the darkness of our guilt and entered the night of eternal death itself as he hung on the cross in our place. Even the sun refused to shine on that sacrifice (Matthew 27:45)! But on Easter morning, the Son of God, the Light of the world, scattered the shadows of our fear and despair forever. Now the Son-shine of forgiveness and peace belong to God's people forever! Praise him!

— **TO SAVOR** —

Keep Easter morning in mind as you read and reread today's verse, and consider the light this truth shines into any dark situations you may face today.

So do not fear, for I am with you; do not be dismayed,
for I am your God.

Isaiah 41:10

— **TO FLAVOR** —

Cinnamon can be used either whole or ground into a powder. Its uses vary in cultures across the world; however, North Americans most often use it as a dessert spice in cakes, puddings, pies, cookies, or any treats made with apples.

~Rosemary

Day 17

And hope does not disappoint us.

Romans 5:5

When I taught preschoolers, I tried each year to give my students the joy of watching a monarch butterfly emerge from its chrysalis. The children took great delight in the beauty of this miracle, as did I. The caterpillar would shed its striped skin to begin its transformation into the pupa stage, which looked like a jade green vase with gold pin dots. In as little as two weeks, the green coloration would turn transparent and the butterfly would begin to emerge, squeezing itself through a tiny opening. Once out, it looked feeble and weak until its wings inflated and stiffened.

At first the children would express disappointment and even dismay because the butterfly could not fly. But I could assure them with all certainty that they simply needed to have patience, to wait with hope. And every time, their hope-filled waiting did not disappoint. Eventually each year, we would together let the butterfly fly away.

So it is with us. Though we may sometimes doubt it, hope anchored in Christ does not disappoint. Yes, there will be times of waiting. Yes, there will be times of struggle. Yes, there will be times of weakness. And, yes, at times we will wait days, months, or even years in hope for the transformation our Savior has promised.

But each time we can wait in trust, in thanksgiving and hope. And as God's promises prove true, time after time, we grow in trust that one day we will shed the chrysalis of this present life and emerge victorious in our Lord's presence in heaven. Relying on our Savior's love and trusting his sacrifice on Calvary's cross, we will not be disappointed.

TO SAVOR

In the Greek of the New Testament, the word *transformed* found in today's verse is the word from which we derive the English word *metamorphosis*. Just as our Creator transforms caterpillars into butterflies, so the Holy Spirit transforms us into the very image of Christ! What—specifically—is he working on in your heart and mind today?

> *Do not conform any longer to the pattern of this world, but be transformed by the renewing of your mind.*
>
> Romans 12:2

TO FLAVOR

Cumin has a taste that can best be described as fiery. This aromatic spice fires up American chili, Indian dishes, and Mexican specialties. You will often also find it in recipes that include lamb, eggplant, or tomatoes.

~Rosemary

Day 18

... because God has poured out his love ...

Romans 5:5

Each time I see a waterfall, I am silenced—both by the sheer beauty of God's creation and by the symbolism water carries in the Scriptures. As God created our world, he made water a necessity of life. As scientists today consider the possibility of life on other planets, they look first for evidence of water on those planets. The absence of water makes the existence of life much, much less likely.

Paul writes in Romans 5:5, "God has poured out his love." This phrase describes no miserly trickle! Rather, it calls to mind a mighty waterfall, a roaring, perpetual geyser! God has poured out his love for us in our Savior, Jesus.

It's not by accident that Jesus said to the woman at the well, "The water I give them takes away thirst altogether. It becomes a perpetual spring within them, giving them eternal life" (John 4:14 NLT). Nor is it accidental that the woman then exclaimed, "Give me this water!" (John 4:15).

God poured out his love when he sent his Son to live the perfect life we could not live, to die the death we deserved in punishment for our sins, and to rise from death victorious forever. Recalling his sacrifice, let God's love and grace continually wash over you, cleansing you in the flood of forgiveness and unconditional love Jesus earned for you on Calvary. Then live out that love in joyful confidence.

TO SAVOR

Each time you turn on the faucet today, think about this verse and let God's love, poured out for you in Christ Jesus, refresh you.

For all of you who were baptized into Christ have clothed yourselves with Christ.

Galatians 3:27

TO FLAVOR

Dill seeds have a taste that resembles dill leaves. But they also taste a bit like caraway. Most often used to flavor dill pickles, this herb can also flavor other pickled fruits and vegetables.

—*Rosemary*

Day 19

. . . into our hearts . . .

Romans 5:5

How's your heart? From commercials for cholesterol-lowering drugs to articles dealing with heart-healthy nutrition to books urging daily rigorous exercise, heart care advice floods in upon us, seemingly from every side.

But what about the health of our spiritual hearts? In Proverbs 4:20–23, Solomon wisely urges,

Pay attention to what I say; listen closely to my words.
Do not let them out of your sight, keep them within your heart;
for they are life to those who find them and health to a man's whole
body. Above all else, guard your heart, for it is the wellspring of life.

Whatever we pour into our hearts, the same will come pouring out. So what are you pouring into your heart? Jesus teaches, "For out of the overflow of the heart the mouth speaks" (Matthew 12:34). Perhaps what you see spilling out from your heart and overflowing from your lips disappoints or even appalls you. Perhaps you see evidence that lovelessness clogs your spiritual arteries. Perhaps your worship or your prayer life betrays a heart cool toward your Lord and hardened toward his promises.

If these diagnostic signs alarm you, take heart. Jesus has poured out his heart in love for you on his own cross. Through faith in his sacrifice, you are forgiven. You are loved. You are alive. Open your heart to his Word of grace and you will be filled with joy. Then exercise that love freely as you care for those around you in Jesus' name.

------------------------------ **TO SAVOR** ------------------------------

As you ponder the wonder of your Savior's love for you today, let these words guide your thoughts:

A heart at peace gives life to the body.

Proverbs 14:30

------------------------------ **TO FLAVOR** ------------------------------

Fennel seeds taste a lot like anise seeds; the two can almost be used interchangeably. An important ingredient in Italian and Greek cooking, fennel seed also often appears in Chinese, Indian, and Egyptian recipes.

~Rosemary

Day 20

. . . by the Holy Spirit, whom he has given us . . .

Romans 5:5

Years ago, I was caught in a blinding blizzard as I drove on the Interstate. A whiteout! Winds whipped the fast-falling snow across the road, creating conditions that made it impossible to see further than a few feet beyond my front bumper. I felt quickly disoriented, then soon lost! To my relief, the taillights of a truck appeared directly in front of me, and I followed them through the blinding snow to safety.

As we travel through this often stormy life, when we find ourselves feeling confused or even lost in our circumstances, when we don't know where to turn, we can turn to our Savior-God. He promises:

> *Whether you turn to the right or to the left, your ears will hear a voice behind you, saying, "This is the way; walk in it."*
>
> *Isaiah 30:21*

No matter how confusing the issues we face or how complex our choices grow, we know for sure that our Lord will lead us along the paths of Spirit-created fruitfulness, along paths of love, joy, peace, patience, kindness, goodness, faithfulness, gentleness, and self-control (Galatians 5:22–23).

Are you trying desperately to find peace and hope? It is already yours—by the power of the Spirit within you. Give up trying to find your own way. Follow the Savior's lead and he will provide all that you need.

TO SAVOR

As you take one step after the next today, think about this verse from the pen of the apostle Paul:

Since we live by the Spirit, let us keep in step with the Spirit.

Galatians 5:25

TO FLAVOR

Ginger is sometimes sold fresh as a root ready for grinding and sometimes dried in its already-ground form. It appears often in recipes for baked goods, but it can also be combined with pickling spices and in blends to flavor various meats. Recipes from Thailand and other cultures of the Far East often include this spice.

~Rosemary

Spoon, Don't Sprinkle

TO FLAVOR

You do it; I do it; we all do it. We take the jar of herbs or spices, hold it over the steaming dish we are cooking, and sprinkle the herb or spice right from the container into the pot. It's easy. It's quick. But beware: You may be sacrificing the flavor of the spice that remains in the spice jar—all for the sake of saving a few seconds.

Rather than shaking spices from their container right into the simmering pot, take the time to measure the right amounts into a spoon or even into your hand before adding them. If you don't, the rising steam will often make what's left lose its flavor or clump together. (Ahhh . . . so that's what happened, you are saying to yourself!)

In the same way an experienced cook knows how to deliver just the right measure of herbs or spices to the kettle and, in doing so, preserve the rest, so God knows how to send just the wisdom and guidance we need as we encounter the circumstances of life. The secret for us lies in trusting him to preserve us as he continues to use us productively, both now and into the future, according to his will.

TO SAVOR

Think about yourself in regard to your family, your friends, your place of work, and your place of play. What are your strengths? How might God use these to honor and glorify him? Are you resting and otherwise caring for yourself to make that service continually possible? Reflect on your answers to these questions as you journal in the space below.

_____

_____

_____

_____

_____

_____

_____

_____

_____

_____

_____

FOR THE SAVIOR

Lord, transform my life by the renewing of my mind. Show me your ways and teach me your paths so that my hope might be in you. Let me walk in the light of your love. In Jesus' precious name. Amen.

Day 21

God demonstrates his own love for us in this . . .

Romans 5:8

I live in Missouri. Every time I notice a license plate on the car in front of me, it reminds me I live in the "show-me" state. I suspect that the citizens of my state aren't the only ones with this attitude. Don't most people tend to rally around the cry: "Don't just tell me . . . show me!"? Well, God does just that . . . he tells us *and* he shows us everything we need to live lives pleasing to him and satisfying for us.

First, our Lord communicates his holy, irrevocable Law. He once etched that Law onto stone tablets as he delivered the Ten Commandments to Moses. The Scriptures tell us many times that our Creator has also etched that Law onto every human heart (for example, Psalm 40:8). We all know in the depth of our being the rightness of that Law:

> *Love the Lord your God with all your heart and with all your soul and with all your mind and with your strength. . . . Love your neighbor as yourself.*
>
> Mark 12:30–31

But when we face ourselves honestly, we know each and every day that we fall far short of doing what the Law tells us. So then God shows us the Gospel! He did that when he sent his Son, Jesus, to do the Law-keeping we could not do on our own. Jesus kept God's Law perfectly for us, in our place.

God demonstrates his great love for us day by day as he reminds us of the Good News of forgiveness and salvation in Christ. And as he does that, he also gives us the faith to believe it. He works in us the strength we need to respond to his love with thankful hearts and holy lives. In the most beautiful way possible, God turned "show and tell" upside down and backwards. Now he "tells and shows" us his love, his great love for us in Christ Jesus!

TO SAVOR

Find rest and peace today as you read and reread, think and rethink the glorious truths in these words:

> *Through Jesus the forgiveness of sins is proclaimed to you. Through him everyone who believes is justified from everything you could not be justified from by the law of Moses.*
>
> *Acts 13:38–39*

TO FLAVOR

Nutmeg, grated and speckled, looks as delightful as it tastes. Cooking stores often carry nutmeg graters, but any small grater will do. Nutmeg adds an enchanting flavor to many desserts, especially cakes, cookies, puddings, custards, and pies.

Day 22

While we were still sinners . . .

Romans 5:8

How many times have you heard someone shout or pout, "Life's just not fair"? In reality, this statement is unequivocally true . . . and we ought to be eternally grateful!

After all, if life were truly fair, it would mean that we would get from God exactly what we deserve. Not a pretty picture! Not something any of us truly wants! Even the apostle Paul—who experienced one of the most dramatic spiritual U-turns of all times, a turnaround from persecutor to believer—writes about his own struggle with sin in Romans 7:18–19:

> *I know that nothing good lives in me, that is, my sinful nature. For I have the desire to do what is good, but I cannot carry it out. For what I do is not the good I want to do; no, the evil I do not want to do—this I keep on doing.*

You and I know all about Paul's struggle. It's our struggle too! We cannot escape from our sinful nature (Romans 7:19). We act it out in every harmful thing we do and say and think. As C. S. Lewis once pointed out, we are not sinners because we occasionally sin. Rather, we commit occasional sins because we are, at heart, always sinners!

The burden of that truth pushed Paul to cry out in frustration, "What a wretched man I am! Who will rescue me from this body of death?" (Romans 7:24). Perhaps you've felt that same kind of frustration at times. Worse still, Romans 6:23 points us toward the awful consequences we deserve because of our own sin: "For the wages of sin is death."

But, thanks be to God, the verse does not end there. Instead, it continues: "but the gift of God is eternal life in Christ Jesus our Lord." Through faith in Jesus, we do *not* get what we deserve. Through faith in Jesus, we receive life instead! Eternal life! Aren't you thankful that life *is not* fair?

TO SAVOR

Find joy and peace in God's gift of eternal life as you meditate now on these beloved words:

> *For God so loved the world that he gave his one and only Son, that whoever believes in him shall not perish but have eternal life.*

> *John 3:16*

TO FLAVOR

Paprika in each of its many varieties adds a kick to any recipe. But beware! A smidgen of hot paprika will flavor a lot of food! Cooks around the world add paprika to a variety of recipes. Try sprinkling it on fried potatoes or macaroni and cheese.

Day 23

Christ died . . .

Romans 5:8

A beautiful statue of Christ stands high on the altar of the church in which I worshiped while I grew up. Perhaps you've seen a statue like it: Christ stands with his head bowed and his hands extended, scarred for all to see.

From childhood on, those scars on Christ's hands and feet have mesmerized me. But I was well into adulthood before I truly realized the impact they have made on me. Though just an artist's image, the scars on that statue remind me in a stark, emotion-laden way of the real scars my Savior bore for me . . . the sacrifice of true love he made for me.

To this day, when I look at those scars, I realize how fully I've messed up my life—how focused I've been on my own agenda, my own needs. How I've hurt others and been slow to forgive those who have hurt me. How I've failed to live up to the expectations of others, let alone the expectations of God. And in my longing to be loved in spite of my failures, the scars remind me that I am truly cherished because of the precious blood my Savior shed so that my sins could be forgiven. Jesus hung on Calvary's cross for me. For me! And he hung there for you, too!

Isn't it funny how often we cross our fingers, hoping for the best, when the very best is already ours because of the cross of Christ? Our real hope lies there—and only there—in life and in death.

TO SAVOR

Cherish your Savior's sacrifice for you as you worship him for the wonders revealed in these words of Scripture:

And he died for all, that those who live should no longer live for themselves but for him who died for them and was raised again.

2 Corinthians 5:15

TO FLAVOR

Pepper turns up in dishes around the world. It transcends cultures, prized for the heat it adds to each dish. Whole peppercorns keep their flavor longer than ground; therefore, whole peppercorns work best in stews, soups, and other recipes that call for simmering.

—Lemongrass

Day 24

. . . for us.

Romans 5:8

In creation, God gave women a nurturing spirit that seeks to celebrate, affirm, and encourage. We tend to live, "One for all and all for one." When something sad happens to another, we share in that sadness. And when something delightful happens to us, we long for others to share in the joy.

Well, the greatest thing to ever happen to us was most certainly done by one . . . for all. Christ died and rose again, not only for me, but also for you . . . and for everyone who has ever lived or will ever live on this earth. He didn't die only for me . . . he died for *us.*

Do you know someone who is hurting, living with the consequences of past mistakes and longing to be free? someone who does not know about the Savior's love? Do you know others who have already heard of God's great love for them in Christ, but need to be reminded of his pardon, who need to feel arms of love wrapped around them? By the power of the Holy Spirit, God's gift of grace has been released *to* you, and it is also released *through* you. God can and will use you to draw those who are hurting closer to himself.

While it is true that God loves you as if you were the only person who ever existed, he also loves every other person on earth to that same, infinite degree. The message of "one for all" opens the path to peace, comfort, hope, and healing. And it's too good to keep secret.

TO SAVOR

Today's words from Scripture proclaim profound truth so simply, but with such power:

[Christ] died for all.

2 Corinthians 5:15

TO FLAVOR

Turmeric turns everything that it touches yellow, bringing with it a slightly bitter taste. Only a little will fully flavor beans and lentils, rice, tomatoes, broccoli, and fish.

Day 25

Therefore, since we have been justified through faith,
we have peace with God through our Lord Jesus Christ, through whom
we have gained access by faith into this grace in which we now stand.
And we rejoice in the hope of the glory of God.
Not only so, but we also rejoice in our sufferings, because we know that
suffering produces perseverance; perseverance, character; and character,
hope. And hope does not disappoint us, because God has poured out his
love into our hearts by the Holy Spirit, whom he has given us. . . .
God demonstrates his own love for us in this:
While we were still sinners, Christ died for us.

Romans 5:1-8

Think about it: Only Christ can turn a crust of bread into a banquet. For those who know him as Savior and Friend, mere existence becomes life everlasting.

No matter how good my life or yours might be, while we remain on this earth, life will always include dry times, crusty days, days filled with disappointment, pain, struggle, and strife. Sometimes we even build a crust around ourselves, a crust of despair or hurt that no one but God can penetrate. And that he does . . . by the Savior's love.

The banquet that awaits us in heaven defies all human comprehension. Sin and death have spoiled life here on earth; our planet and each culture it has spawned will eventually end up on the scrap heap of eternity. How sad! But for those who believe in Christ as Savior, the end of life here becomes the passageway to

SAVORING GOD'S LOVE

eternal joy. For believers, the grave stands as the foyer of life face-
to-face with our Lord.

God intends that we truly savor that kind of divine love. He
invites us here and now on earth to "taste and see that the LORD is
good" (Psalm 34:8). And even as we do, he reminds us that it is
but a foretaste of the feast to come.

TO SAVOR

Think about that eternal banquet prepared for you as you ponder
this promise from your Savior:

> *[Jesus said,] I tell you the truth, whoever hears my word and believes
> in him who sent me has eternal life and will not be condemned; he
> has crossed over from death to life.*

John 5:24

~Lemongrass

An Herb Garden of Your Own?

TO FLAVOR

After learning more about using herbs and spices, you may be tempted to grow your own. That sounds like a splendid idea!

But before you begin, take a trip to your local library or bookstore and learn all you can about how to create optimal conditions for herb gardening. Herbs differ, for example, in their need for light and moisture. You will want to plan carefully for best results.

Growing herbs most certainly need light and water. Light and water also play a critical role in a growing faith. Several times the Scriptures call Christ the Light of the world. He is the light that shines through the dark brokenness of sin. Jesus is also the water of life who invites: "If anyone is thirsty, let him come to me and drink" (John 7:37).

Light and water—herbs cannot grow without them. And we cannot thrive and grow in faith without the same from our Lord. He quenches our thirst and lights our way . . . from the first taste to the last, from here to eternity. Savor his love always.

TO SAVOR

Write a prayer or a poem of praise, expressing the thanks in your heart today for Jesus, your Light and your Refreshment.

_____

_____

_____

_____

_____

_____

_____

_____

_____

_____

_____

_____

_____

_____

FOR THE SAVIOR

Lord, help me never forget that you know me, love me, forgive me, and comfort me. Flavor my life with your grace so that I will always savor your love for me. To your glory and in your name, Jesus. Amen.

Taste and see that the LORD is good.

Psalm 34:8